ideals
OLD-FASHIONED

I'm just a bit old-fashioned,
In spite of modern ways,
And wish I could have been around
In the good old-fashioned days.

There's far more charm in twisted lanes
Along our countryside,
Than all the modern super-roads
That stretch so far and wide.

So I'd rather be old-fashioned
In a few things here and there,
And try to keep old-fashioned charm
An everyday affair.

Carice Williams

ISBN 0-8249-1043-5

Publisher, Patricia A. Pingry
Editor, Ramona Richards
Art Director, David Lenz
Permissions, Kathleen Gilbert
Copy Editor, Susan DuBois
Phototypesetter, Angela Smith

IDEALS—Vol. 43, No. 4 June MCMLXXXVI IDEALS (ISSN 0019-137X) is published eight times a year, February, March, May, June, August, September, November, December
by IDEALS PUBLISHING CORPORATION, Nelson Place at Elm Hill Pike, Nashville, Tenn. 37214-8000
Second class postage paid at Nashville, Tennessee, and additional mailing offices.
Copyright© MCMLXXXVI by IDEALS PUBLISHING CORPORATION.
POSTMASTER: Send address changes to Ideals, Post Office Box 148000, Nashville, Tenn. 37214-8000
All rights reserved. Title IDEALS registered U.S. Patent Office.
Published simultaneously in Canada.

SINGLE ISSUE—$3.50
ONE-YEAR SUBSCRIPTION—eight consecutive issues as published—$15.95
TWO-YEAR SUBSCRIPTION—sixteen consecutive issues as published—$27.95
Outside U.S.A., add $4.00 per subscription year for postage and handling.

Front and back covers from H. Armstrong Roberts

Inside front cover from H. Armstrong Roberts
Inside back cover by Fred Sieb

W9-BRS-520

An Old-Fashioned Garden

Give me an old-fashioned garden
   With hollyhocks and rambler rose,
A trellis with a seat beneath
   Where honeysuckle grows.

Give me a fountain bird bath
   Where warblers come to play
And tarry for a while to sing
   A little roundelay.

Give me a summer afternoon
   With butterflies and bees
Sipping honey from the flowers,
   While zephyrs stir the trees.

Give me soft, fleecy clouds
   Adrift in azure skies.
Give me all these and I will be
   Quite close to paradise.

Gladys Harp

The Hummingbird

Poised with iridescent grace
In puzzling, mystic flight,
The hummingbird drank from a rose
To sate his appetite.

Ethereal flash of tiny might
With ruby on his breast,
He eyed me with a jet-black eye
And gold upon his crest.

Then, rising on a summer breeze,
His glowing wings outspread,
He took my heart upon his back
And vanished overhead!

Stella Craft Tremble

Wood Thrush

I hear your haunting, lovely song
Within the woods at close of dusk.
Your song that sings of things I love:
Of scented rose and woodland musk;

Of ferns beside a winding brook,
White honeysuckle in the rain;
Of meadow daisies in the sun
Along a blossom-haunted lane.

Wood thrush, I marvel as I hear
The beauty of your silver tongue!
No day is ever lost for me
When your sweet vesper hymn is sung.

William Arnette Wofford

Readers' Reflections

Nature

Sittin' in the shadows
On a lazy summer night.
Crickets jumpin' here and there;
Fireflies in jagged flight.

A frog's a-callin' from the creek;
An owl hoots from a tree.
Locusts chirp their weary song;
Night winds whistle free.

The moon's a-playin' hide-and-seek;
The leaves caress the sky.
The brook's a-hummin' sweet love songs
To the mountains oh, so high.

A raindrop plays on the tip of a rose;
The birds have ceased their callin'.
Nature's put herself to bed
And darkness now is fallin'.

Sonja J. Haddox
Chillicothe, OH

The Old Country Store

The wooden sign, through years of wear,
Listed the goods we bought with care.
Mixing whisks to butter molds,
Iron stoves for when you're cold.

Sorghum for a syrup cake,
Wooden handles for an old leaf rake.
Blue pie plates and strong pine tar,
Honey in a green glass jar.

Biscuit pans and meat cutters,
Churns for making country butter.
Molasses kegs and one for pickles,
Saw blades and curving sickles.

Natural soap and soil test kits,
Cherry pitters and bridle bits.
Aladdin lamps and grinding mills,
Boxes of Lydia Pinkum pills.

Gingham bolts of calico,
Crystal buttons in a row.
Chewing tobacco and peppermint sticks,
Soda crackers and hard rock picks.

The old country store for kith and kin,
We'll settle our bill when the crops come in!

Elisabeth Weaver Winstead
Nashville, TN

Photo Overleaf
CALIFORNIA DAISIES
Ed Cooper

Early June Morn

It's early on a soft, June morn.
A fresh new day, which is the norm.
In the garden, all is growing;
In the yard, the grass needs mowing.

On the fence, red roses climb.
A redbird whistles in the pine.
The sun slants through the hardwood trees;
I feel the whisper of a breeze;

It sets the windchimes jing-a-linging.
In the meadow, a lark is singing.
I hear the cooing mourning dove;
This is the time of day I love.

My yard is filled with lovely sights.
Each morning brings fresh, new delights.
How peaceful it is, and I'm thankful, too,
For each bright, June day God sends anew.

LaVon M. Wood
Benton, LA

Memories

My mind goes back
To the days of old:
Long evening strolls
Down the country road.

The path led to
The sparkling pond
Of which we kids
Were very fond.

With a friend,
We'd walk along.
Share a secret,
Sing a song.

Oh, those days!
I remember them well.
And so many stories
That I could tell!

Lisa Reynolds
Mission Hills, CA

Editor's Note: Readers are invited to submit unpublished poetry, short anecdotes, and humorous reflections on life for possible publication in future *Ideals* issues. Please send copies only; manuscripts will not be returned. Writers will receive $10 for each published submission. Send materials to "Readers' Reflections," Ideals Publishing, Nelson Place at Elm Hill Pike, Nashville, Tennessee 37214.

Old-Fashioned Memories

I came to the homestead at dawning
When the sun was fresh in the sky;
I saw in each room and each corner
Mementos of days long gone by:
A crib, an old wooden cradle,
A carriage, a worn baby quilt,
A teddy bear, faded and ragged,
But stuffed with sweet memories still.

I came to the homestead at noontide
When the sun was high in the sky;
I saw there a treasure of keepsakes,
Reminders of days long gone by:
Some old graduation pictures,
Some old wedding photographs, too.
Memorabilia of yesterdays
When years to us children were new.

I came to the homestead at evening
When the sun was low in the sky,
And I then understood the reason
For treasured days now long gone by.
For there in old-fashioned rockers
Sat Mother and our dear old dad.
I kissed them, then gratefully thanked them
For the wonderful memories I have.

Loise Pinkerton Fritz

Photo Opposite
PFEIFER HOMESTEAD, WYOMING
Gene Ahrens

Six Days Make One Weak

Seven days make one week. But the schedules my mother and grandmother used to keep remind me of an old adage: "six days like this make one weak!"

I grew up before electricity, and the week was as inevitable as death and taxes and neither was allowed to interfere.

Wash on Monday, iron on Tuesday,
Clean on Wednesday, mend on Thursday,
Hoe on Friday, bake on Saturday,
Rest on Sunday, wash on Monday.

Monday. When I got up for school on Monday, signs of the washing to follow were already evident. The wood cookstove was blazing. Twin galvanized boilers were steaming. Work clothes were soaking. Bleach and bluing assailed my nostrils as I ate breakfast, eyeing the big bar of hard yellow scrub soap and the wringer it took two of us to turn when overalls went through.

After school I helped hang clothes on the strong steel wires strung between two posts or two young trees. I could also count on having at least two fingers "bitten" by those spring-loaded clothespins. None of the slip-on type that could also slip off and drop clothes to the ground! We propped the lines in the middle with a sapling when we did blankets and heavy clothes. In winter, they "freeze-dried" until the long underwear stood by itself in the kitchen. Of course, summer snapped them so dry they had to be sprinkled and rolled for hours.

Tuesday. Another raging fire, this time with three "sad irons" heating. A wooden clamp-on handle, a wet finger sizzling against the bottom, and they were ready! Everything was starched, and the number of shirts and blouses I scorched before learning the fine art of ironing equalled the national debt!

Wednesday was cleaning day. Saturdays got a lick and promise but Wednesdays! Ceilings, floors, walls, windows. More boilers of hot water. Suds, wax, aching backs and pride of work well done. Wednesday suppers were usually stews racy with onions, or a pot of beans cooked on the back of the stove. There wasn't time for "fancies" on Wednesdays.

Thursday we mended. Our overalls had patches on the patches, and I can still see Mom with her overflowing basket of socks that were interwoven with soft yarn. No lumpy darns in our socks. Our grimy feet playing in the dust proudly wore those mended stockings.

Friday released us to the garden. Little fingers learned early to differentiate between weeds and vegetables, at least most of the time! Working together as a family, it didn't seem hard, especially when we knew punch and cookies waited as a reward.

Saturday was a fun day. Our world was one that took seriously the admonition, "Thou shalt rest on Sunday, and keep it holy." Saturday was the preparation day. Pies, cakes, set salads. The pantry was filled. And

Sunday without company was like rain without water. From ten to twenty-five, who knew? The more people who conveniently "dropped in" for dinner, the more jars of pickles, jams and home-canned vegetables came out of our "root house" to supplement our Saturday baking.

Saturday night was also bath night. Daily sponge baths kept us neat, but Saturday night we "soaked." Ground-in elbow and heel dirt was attacked. The biggest washtub was filled with water and even on the coldest winter nights provided comfort. We dried in huge towels, wrapped ourselves in flannel pajamas and robes and sat in front of the living room wood heater, turning like roasts on spits before racing for bed and mounds of heavy, homemade quilts.

Sunday was church and rest. Yet there were also other people around, with everyone helping prepare meals and do dishes afterwards. The best dishes. Linen tablecloth instead of oilcloth. Years later Mom and Dad used Sunday afternoon for drives and dinner out. It must have been a welcome change from the busy Sundays at home after hectic "weaks"!

Now, in the middle of "brownouts" and "blackouts," I mentally run through the same work schedule my mother and grandmothers followed—but what a difference!

Washday is any day. Toss 'em in a washer, change to a dryer. You can wash any time. No pumping or heating of water, no chopping and stoking a stove, no carrying off buckets of water afterwards.

Ironing. Who irons? Once over lightly on Perma-Press does it all.

Cleaning. Still exists and yet:

Vacuum cleaners for the floors with rugs.

Damp mops for no-wax floors without rugs.

Windows, walls, furniture? New and convenient attachments for them all.

Mending. A lost art.

Hoeing and weeding seem a little ridiculous when vegetables can be purchased from a supermarket for less than it takes to grow them. Cans on shelves have replaced battalions of jars in the cellar.

Baking. Mom and I still bake, but in an electric oven after mixing with an electric beater. I have to admit, I kind of miss adding one stick of wood at a time to keep the fire even, and turning the pans so we wouldn't get "lopsided layers" from an oven that was hotter on one side than the other.

Even Sundays aren't the same. I remember being bone-tired but content on Saturday nights as I snuggled deep in my bed. Six-day work weeks did make people weak—ready to rest on Sundays.

How ironic now on Saturday night to look back and wonder how I got so tired! With all my "labor-saving" devices, where's all that free time I should have? Those hours of emptiness to dream and scheme?

A few days ago our house was filled with company. Just before nine that night, the lights went off for two hours. It was great! No TV. No stereo. We talked, laughed, and told stories—to the delight of all from four-year-old David to eighty-three-year-old Mom. And I wondered . . .

It is predicted that the time may come when we will have to return to some of the old ways of doing and making do. I shudder at the thought. Yet in my more honest moments I have to admit—six days living in this world of pressure, jets, politics and rising prices, fulfills the old saying more than in my grandmothers' days, and is enough to make anyone weak!

Originally published in *Wyoming Rural Electric News*, January 1983.

Colleen Reece

Summer's Serenade

Oh, how I like to wander
Across the rich green hills.
Summer breezes kiss my brow,
And I find a million thrills.

Many new discoveries,
Where nature gave her best.
Lost seclusions still unmarred,
There I pause and rest.

Let me find my solitude,
And I can reminisce;
Other places, other times,
Which once were much like this.

Then I wander on again
Along the hidden trail,
Overgrown by brush and grass,
With tiny flowers frail.

Let my eyes find the wonder:
Great things that nature's made,
And I will find contentment,
In summer's serenade!

Anton J. Stoffle

Photo Opposite
HAY RAKE
Fred Sieb

The Old General Store

"For Sale" read the sign on the time-
    warped door
That opened to joys of the old general store.
It stood on the corner, where four country roads
Crossed hands, in a village where
    kindliest folks
Flashed smiles and spoke greetings when
    entering the door
To buy this or that at the old general store.

"This" or "that" was the merchandise sold;
Item on item, the number untold,
Comprising the stock in the old general store
Where so often we passed through its time-
    weathered door
To purchase, perchance, a kerosene lamp,
Some barrel molasses or a postage stamp.
High-top shoes before start of school,
Colorful thread on large or small spools.
Perhaps penny candy in a glass-covered case.
Anise sticks, licorice—whiche'er pleased
    the taste
Of children who had but a penny to spend
On a favorite candy to share with a friend.

"For Sale" read the sign on the time-
    beaten door
That opened to joys of the old general store
Where, tucked in each basket of victuals sold,
Was a bit of good cheer worth its weight
    in gold.
And though progress has felled this old
    country store,
We still glimpse its treasures through
    memory's door.

Loise Pinkerton Fritz

The Gibson Girl: An American Ideal

From the mid-1890s to the early 1920s, the Gibson Girl symbolized the ideal American woman. Her creator was illustrator Charles Dana Gibson (1867-1944), whose pen and ink drawings portrayed the "emerging woman" at the turn of the century: attractive, athletic, poised, and intelligent. The Gibson Girl served as the model for a generation of American women—urban and rural—who attempted to copy the Gibson Girl's dress and character.

Gibson's drawings were first published in *Life* in 1892, but it was not until 1894 that the Gibson Girl became the rage of New York. In that year, the illustrator's first collection of Gibson Girls was published. His drawings reflected various situations in American life and involved seven distinct types of females: the Beauty, the Boy-Girl, the Flirt, the Sentimental, the Convinced, the Ambitious, and the Well-Balanced.

Each of the Gibson Girls had a strong, independent personality. Gibson thought of the Boy-Girl as a "good-fellow" sort, who was a sport and enjoyed the excitement of nearly losing her life on a runaway horse more than the attention of a love-sick man. He described the Convinced as the Gibson Girl who set a certain goal and pursued it without taking a single sidestep. Gibson's favorite type, the Well-Balanced, illustrated the female who was all harmony and easily balanced all aspects of contemporary life. This type came nearest to a romantic bachelor's "ideal of young American womanhood."

Gibson's cartoons, as he called his drawings, were satires of American society at the turn of the century. The Gibson Girl's appearance was a breath of fresh air and was met with overwhelming acceptance. Her popularity spread quickly across the country. She was a regular feature in such widely read publications as *Collier's Weekly*, *Century*, and *Harper's*. By 1900, Gibson Girls were included in *Leslie's Weekly*, the forerunner of today's picture magazines, and in the avant-garde *Ladies Home Journal*, whose writers exposed social injustices and promoted worthy civic causes. The beginning of the new century also found Gibson Girls in major European periodicals, and the illustrator's works soon were collected in several books, including *The American* (1900), *The Social Ladder* (1902), and *The Gibson Book* (1906).

The public popularity of the Gibson Girl was totally unexpected by artist Charles Dana Gibson. His motive in creating the unique character had been to offer humorous comments on American life, and he was surprised when the Gibson Girl became a national fad. Artists all over the country began to imitate

Gibson's drawing, and copies of the Gibson Girl soon appeared on silk handkerchiefs, china plates, hardwood easels, and leather items. The Gibson Girl was included in the cast of early vaudeville shows, and her name was given to the shirtwaist, the pompadour, and a type of riding crop.

The Gibson Girl's success was a reflection of the times. America was rapidly changing as women entered the public work force, and women were eager for a new image. The Gibson Girl conveyed the message that women could have freedom and individuality while remaining feminine. Her casual costume was evidence of new-found freedom, since the cotton shirtwaist and skirt were less hampering than the established fashion of elaborate silk dresses with frills and uncomfortable bustles.

As the shirtwaist and skirt caught the fancy of American women, those garments joined cotton underwear and kimonos to become the first mass-produced women's clothing. Workers in middle Atlantic factories produced shirtwaists and skirts patterned after the Gibson Girl costume. New York City, where the costumes were designed and marketed, became one of the world's major clothing centers.

During the first decade of the twentieth century, shirtwaists took on new dimensions. From humble beginnings as simple blouses with little decoration, shirtwaists were expanded to offer a variety of styles which were tucked, beribboned, lace-trimmed, or wide-cuffed, with a pointed collar or high neckband. White cotton fabric was dyed bright colors and many embroidered designs were added. Tiny pearl buttons marched down the front or back plackets and accented the cuffs. Accessories usually worn with the shirtwaist included a delicate cameo broach or a tiny ladies' watch suspended on a thin gold chain.

When World War I (1914-1918) ushered shortages into America, the Gibson Girl shirtwaists and skirts—which had become almost as elaborate as the earlier silk and taffeta dresses—became too expensive to manufacture. Less expensive and simpler apparel was needed for the country's working women. As the second decade of the twentieth century drew to a close, the "boyish" look became the fashion. Dresses were made of minimal fabric yardage, hanging straight and unfitted, with hemlines at or just above the knees. Pompadour hairstyles were replaced by short, curly styles, and waist-length strings of pearls replaced the old-fashioned cameos. The Roaring Twenties ushered in the Flapper and brought an abrupt end to the Gibson Girl era.

Although the work of Gibson appeared in many books and magazines, and he was in great demand as a portrait painter the last twenty years of his life, he remains best known for his Gibson Girl. The Gibson Girl's national popularity and imitation were outstanding examples of life copying art, and Charles Dana Gibson was one of few persons who enjoyed the accomplishment of having created an American ideal.

Ilene J. Cornwell

Painting Overleaf
THE GENERAL STORE
George Hinke

Country Village

Do you see that peaceful valley
Nestled among those purple hills?
There's a friendly little village
Full of people of good will.

There might be twenty families
Round about the country store,
With a path that's clearly visible
To each neighbor's back door.

Let's look in on the grocer
With his supply of rural needs,
As he chats with his customers
While he's weighing sugar or seeds.

He has crackers in the barrel,
Big round cheeses in the case,
Spools of thread in different colors,
Baby ribbon and pretty lace.

Jars of jelly beans and gumdrops
Sitting out where all can see.
'Tis so tempting to the children
And even grown-ups occasionally.

The little white church across the road
Comes alive each Sunday morn,
When each family gathers there
To worship in prayer and song.

Sunday afternoons are spent
In pitching horseshoes or croquet,
Or maybe sitting under a tree,
Discussing problems of the day.

Now the village is quiet and peaceful,
And each household's safe for the night,
But the morrow will bring activity
When the sun comes into sight.

Ah, this lovely, peaceful valley
Gives forth a beauty to behold!
Lulled by the tranquil quietness,
It's a solace to one's soul.

Ruby Pearl Coffman

Old-Fashioned Breads

Hunter's Bread
Makes 2 loaves

5 to 5½ cups flour, divided
2 packages active dry yeast
1 cup milk
1 cup water
½ cup molasses
2 teaspoons salt
2 tablespoons vegetable oil
1 cup wheat cereal, uncooked
  Vegetable oil

Stir together 2 cups flour and both packages yeast in a large bowl. Combine milk, water, molasses, salt and vegetable oil in a large pan. Place over low heat (120° to 130°) until warm. Add liquid ingredients to flour mixture; beat until smooth, about 3 minutes on high using an electric mixer. Stir in cereal and beat 1 minute. Set aside for 5 minutes. Cover dough and set aside for 45 minutes. Divide dough in half and shape into 2 loaves. Place dough into 2 greased 4½x8-inch pans. Brush with oil. Set aside in a warm place until doubled in size, about 1 hour. Preheat oven to 400°. Bake for 35 to 40 minutes. If needed, cover loaves with foil during last 15 minutes of baking to prevent excessive browning. Remove immediately from pans and brush with oil. Cool on wire racks.

Whole-Wheat Bread
Makes 1 loaf

2 packages active dry yeast
¾ cup warm water
1¼ cups buttermilk
1½ cups flour
3 cups whole-wheat flour, divided
¼ cup shortening
2 tablespoons sugar
2 teaspoons baking powder
2 teaspoons salt
  Softened butter *or* margarine

Dissolve yeast in warm water in a large mixing bowl. Add buttermilk, flour, 1 cup whole-wheat flour, shortening, sugar, baking powder and salt. Using an electric mixer, blend 30 seconds on low speed, scraping bowl constantly while blending. Beat 2 minutes on medium speed, scraping bowl occasionally. Blend in remaining whole-wheat flour. (Dough should remain soft and sticky.) Turn dough onto well-floured board; knead 5 minutes, or about 200 turns. Roll dough into an 18x9-inch rectangle. Roll up, beginning at short side. With side of hand, press each end to seal. Fold ends under loaf. Place loaf seam-side down in a warm place until doubled in size, about 1 hour. Center should rise above pan. Preheat oven to 425°. Bake loaf on a low rack for 30 to 35 minutes. Remove from pan. Brush with butter; cool on wire rack.

Grandma's White Bread
Makes 2 loaves

1 package active dry yeast
¼ cup lukewarm water
2 cups milk, scalded
¼ cup butter *or* margarine
2 tablespoons sugar
2 teaspoons salt
6 cups flour

Sprinkle yeast over lukewarm water. Set aside for 10 minutes; stir to dissolve. Pour hot milk over butter, sugar and salt in a large mixing bowl. Cool to lukewarm; add yeast and 3 cups flour. Beat well; mix in remaining flour. Turn out onto a floured surface; knead until smooth and satiny, about 8 to 10 minutes. Place dough into a greased bowl, turning once to coat both sides. Cover; set aside until doubled in size, about 1½ hours. Punch down; set aside for 30 minutes. Shape into 2 loaves and place into greased 9x5x3-inch pans. Set aside until doubled in size. Preheat oven to 400°. Bake for about 35 minutes or until brown and loaf sounds hollow when tapped.

Taken from *Country Bread Cookbook* by Darlene Kronschnabel, Ideals Publishing, 1978.

Old-Fashioned Things

Do you like old-fashioned things?
Like trolley cars and friendship rings,
Lavender hearts and rose sachets,
Forget-me-nots in sweet bouquets.

Tiny lockets on golden chains,
Gingham checks and weather vanes,
Cameos and lace and pearls—
Do you like old-fashioned girls?

If you like cats and jasmine tea,
Well, just maybe you'll like me.

Elsie Mae Watkins

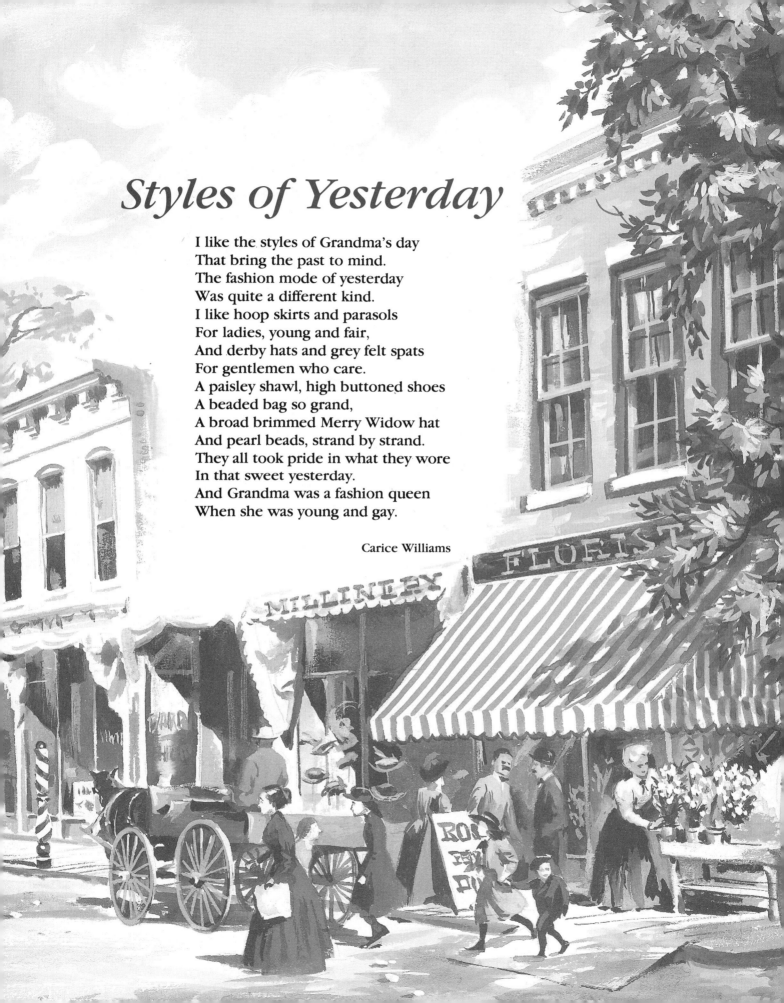

Styles of Yesterday

I like the styles of Grandma's day
That bring the past to mind.
The fashion mode of yesterday
Was quite a different kind.
I like hoop skirts and parasols
For ladies, young and fair,
And derby hats and grey felt spats
For gentlemen who care.
A paisley shawl, high buttoned shoes
A beaded bag so grand,
A broad brimmed Merry Widow hat
And pearl beads, strand by strand.
They all took pride in what they wore
In that sweet yesterday.
And Grandma was a fashion queen
When she was young and gay.

Carice Williams

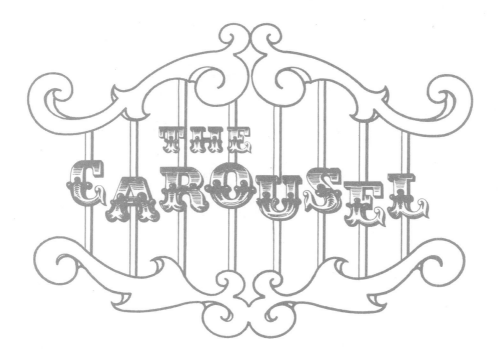

THE CAROUSEL

The horse with the bell on the carousel
Is ever so nice to ride.
Gently we go as he bobs to-and-fro;
I'm never afraid I'll slide.

He has deep brown eyes of the largest size,
His lashes are soft and long,
Round and round he goes, a ring in his nose,
So handsome and brave and strong.

The music plays and the carousel sways,
Faster and faster we speed,
Around and around to the wonderful sound
On my gentle, faithful steed.

I should like to stay on his back all day,
I'd hug him and hold on tight.
We'd have so much fun that when it was done
I'd like to stay on all night!

Viney Wilder Endicott

Photo Opposite
CAROUSEL HORSE
Elaine Reuter

The Proper Thing to Do

Pamela Kennedy

Proper pre-dinner topics of discussion should be limited to five: a child, a picture, an animal, a vase of flowers and a worked ottoman.

Never beat time with your feet or whirl around a chair on one leg.

Kill no vermin such as fleas, lice, ticks, etc. in the sight of others.

The nose should never be fondled before company.

Although the history of a society may be chronicled through its art, its architecture, or its educational systems, the most colorful view of past generations is seen through etiquette. As the tides of social custom ebb and flow, the historical beaches are cluttered with the delightful debris of outdated manners. They are the little bits of flotsam and jetsam that help us define where we are by letting us know where we have been.

Children have always been a target for those pushing manners. Maybe it's because they arrive in such an uncivilized state. Whatever the reason, etiquette books have lots to say to the tykes. Judging from the manners pressed upon children in the eighteenth century, kids haven't changed. They were admonished to "restrain from wriggling . . . hither and thither whilst being spoken to" and to refrain from snickering when listening to an adult botch a joke. Two hundred years later, children are still wriggling and snickering their way through childhood.

At fifteen, young George Washington compiled a list of guidelines for proper behavior. Although centuries old, many of them still provide helpful suggestions for maintaining civility. Here are a few from his list of more than one hundred:

Sleep not when others speak.
Spit not in the fire.
Being set at meat, scratch not, neither spit, cough or blow your nose except there be a necessity for it.
Make no shew of taking great delight in your victuals, neither find fault with what you eat.
Cleanse not your teeth with the table cloth, napkin, fork or knife.
Be not apt to relate news if you know not the truth thereof.

Even though the phrasing may be outdated, following these basic courtesies could certainly stand many of us in good stead today. But these are general guidelines. What about those sticky situations lurking in the social jungle? You may rest assured, for the etiquette books of the past seem to have hit just about every predicament imaginable.

If a lady finds herself in a runaway coach, for example, it is terribly undignified to thrash about in terror and scream. The proper woman will decorously hold her peace, as well as her hat, wait for the vehicle to turn over, relax and roll out!

While excruciatingly correct ladies busied themselves rolling decorously from overturned coaches, well-mannered gents busied themselves with the nuances of hat etiquette. Wearing a hat was no simple matter! Hats were to be worn outdoors, but removed indoors—except, of course, in railway stations. A gentleman always removed his hat during introductions, the playing of the National Anthem and at the passing of the American flag during a parade. Hats were tipped or lifted slightly to acknowledge ladies of refinement. If one was elderly, suffering from arthritis and standing in a stiff wind, he was excused from raising his hat to anyone—regardless of character!

When not busy devising new rules regarding hat tipping, American etiquette experts seemed to invest much time outlining correct feminine behavior. The proper nineteenth century lady never spat in public (one wonders if it was considered acceptable to spit in private), never shook hands with a man, never indulged in double elevation (that was the horrifying habit of lifting *both* sides of the skirt to avoid muddying the hem), and never pretended to have any intelligence whatsoever. On the last point, the guides were most emphatic. Dr. John Gregory, author of *The Ladies Pocket Library,* enjoined his readers to always project a "soft delicacy" and to avoid any attempts at cleverness or serious conversation since "women seldom have materials to furnish a long discourse." If, perchance, an unusual woman had acquired a degree of knowledge, she must "endeavor to keep it a profound secret." Only a century earlier, however, women were expected to keep silent on all topics. One lady who apparently never got the message was immortalized with the following epitaph:

Here lies as silent clay
Miss Arabella Young
Who on the 21st of May
Began to hold her tongue.

Suffice it to say, etiquette has come a long way since then! And though today we can smile with indulgence at the affectations of our ancestors, shake hands with whomever we please and indulge in discussions with members of either sex, etiquette still has its place. Despite the fact that much of it seems without reason, etiquette makes us mindful of others and provides the oil that keeps the gears of society moving smoothly. Perhaps the dichotomy of thought and action that seems to plague social custom was best described by an astute ten-year-old in 1904: "Etiquette," said young Virginia Carey Hudson, "is what you are doing and saying when people are looking and listening. What you are thinking is your business. Thinking is not etiquette."

Country Drug Store

When I was a child, my father and I
Would set out to drive to a village nearby,
Where gaslights burned on each quiet street.
On summer evenings, the people would meet
At the old drug store where the soda clerk
Would mix and measure with flourish and jerk.

As we perched on the wrought iron seats,
We would all partake of incredible sweets;
Butterscotch sundaes and malted milk,
And ice cream sodas as smooth as silk,
As the light was reflected for all who would pass,
From huge colored bottles of red and green glass.

While in the back room, "Doc" mixed up his lotions
And treated the ailing with mystical potions.
I wish sometimes, when the summer is sweet,
That I could go back there and once again meet
With all of the friends who passed through the door
Of that wonderful, magical, country drug store.

Mary Ellen Stelling

The Story of Mr. Moss That Drummer Man

The old-time drummer was the forerunner of the modern-day salesman. This was before automobiles came into commercial use. He would catch a train in Nashville, Tennessee, and get off in McEwen. From the livery stable in McEwen he'd hire a rig which consisted of two horses hitched to a drummer's hack. This was a buggy-like affair with the floorboard in back, lengthened to accommodate baggage. Into this space he piled his sample bags and headed for all the country stores. He mailed a postcard to let the store owner know he'd be there on a certain day. He didn't specify the time of day because he couldn't keep to a close schedule.

Burton James and his father Charles owned and ran a country store two miles from my home, Tumblin' Creek, Tennessee. The coal oil pump stood on the porch near the entrance. On the counter inside was a hoop of cheese, a bottle of pepper sauce and a tobacco cutter. On top of the tobacco cutter was a monkey thumbing his nose. His tail served as a handle. The pepper sauce bottle was filled with Tumblin' Creek bright red hot peppers and vinegar. This sauce was used on all the knick knacks such as Vienna sausages, potted meat, sardines, cheese, pork and beans, etc. For several years I searched for a pepper sauce bottle like the one at Burton James' Store. I found one recently and bought it for three dollars. All soft drinks were called soda pop. There was no ice and they kept the soda pop in a dark room thinking it would stay cool. When you pulled the cap in hot weather, that hot soda pop would shoot out like a roman candle. It was a great day when the drummer man came to Tumblin' Creek. Every boy came to hear the new songs and the latest jokes. They might have been as old as the hills but they were new to us. Let me introduce you to Mr. Moss that Drummer Man.

Richard M. "Pek" Gunn
Poet Laureate of Tennessee

Mister Moss That Drummer Man

Did you ever watch a drummer
Calling on a country store,
And you stood in awe and marveled
As he strode across the floor?

First he drove up in a carriage
That was called a "Drummer's Hack";
Left his panting iron-gray horses
Tied up to the hitching rack.

Took a block of hay and tossed it
To those livery stable nags;
Wrapped his lines around the whipstock
Then brought in his sample bags.

He was wearing pegleg breeches,
Derby hat and button shoes;
Wore a celluloid collar;
Whistled what he called "the blues."

Had a real gold-plated watch fob,
Suspenders branded "Uncle Sam,"
Silk sleeve holders at his elbows,
Cufflinks with his monogram.

Wore a tie of many colors
Tucked within a striped vest;
Smoked a cigar called a "Cremo,"
Known back then as "Tampa's best."

Bought himself some cheese and crackers,
Pork and beans, then Mister Moss
Opened up Vienna sausage;
Flavored it with pepper sauce.

Drank some sudsy warm pop-water;
When he swallowed made a fuss;
The things he bought and ate for dinner
Looked like angel food to us.

Somehow he was always smiling,
Gray eyes twinkled as he spoke;
He just seemed to laugh all over
When he told a funny joke.

He could tell the funniest stories
Make us laugh until we'd cry;
We were glad to see him coming;
Saddened when he said goodby.

I could see he made folks happy.
All their troubles they forgot;
For they talked about the drummer
And did not complain a lot.

Right then I said when I get grown up;
I sure want to if I can;
Make folks happy every day like
Mister Moss that "Drummer Man."

From the book, *Keep on Laughin'* (1975). Reprinted with permission of Tumblin' Creek Enterprises.

Playin' Marbles

A shallow hole was dug in the ground
Anywhere a level place was found.
We used to kneel, our pant knees patched,
In the dirt where a ring was scratched.
Our eyes were trained for careful aim,
To win more marbles was the game.
Yet, the olden game we used to play
Was different than the game today.

If a "shooter" took a peculiar twist,
A turn was lost whenever we missed.
And to lose an "agate" made us fret,
Since good ones often were hard to get.
Under the pillows marbles were kept
To keep them safe whenever we slept.
We often dreamed of winning more
Before a game for keeps was over.

Many years ago when but a lad,
I used to admire the "agates" I had,
For they seemed beautiful to my eyes,
Some good as "shooters," others for size.
There was a favorite, scarred and chipped,
That from my thumb was often flipped,
And in those days, it was really fun
To defeat your opponents, one by one.

If I could find someone to play
A game of marbles the old-fashioned way,
Just for awhile, I would not abstain
From feeling nimble and young again.
I know my aim might not be good,
But I would do the best I could.
And on each "agate" I would blow
To give them luck and lesser glow.

P. F. Freeman

Stored Memories

Among the attic's souvenirs
Grandmother's trunk is there,
Filled with keepsake memories
For all of us to share.
Photographs and a wedding gown
Cover the silver tray,
A book of poems and jewel box
Where pearls and earrings lay.
A blue napkin with silken fringe,
A shawl for the rag doll,
A box of wrappers from candy bars,
With marbles, knife and ball.
Of all these treasures stored away,
Many are dreams of yesterday.

Elisabeth Bouet Bianchi

In Attic Trunks

I love to look through attic trunks,
Lace and memories stored away;
Faded photos, jeweled fans,
Mementos of a by-gone day.

Old valentines and tarnished lockets,
Outdated frocks, a baby's shoe,
A tattered doll, a beadwork bag,
A smelling-jar of gold and blue.

Blurred journals with dried flowers pressed,
Smiles and teardrops packed away,
In crumbling bits of old love letters,
Mementos of a by-gone day.

Elsie Mae Watkins

The Old Shoe Last

My shoes had started wearing out;
They needed mending badly.
I took them to the old wood-house
And showed them to my daddy.

He took my shoes and smiled a bit,
Then said, "What an awful task!"
But I knew he didn't care too much;
He sort of liked the old shoe last.

I watched him quickly get it out,
Then square himself upon a seat,
And shape thick leather to the sole—
Much like a tune his hammer beat.

The thing I liked the very best
Was when he trimmed the edges 'round.
The job was done and my shoes seemed new.
My feet no longer touched the ground!

Zelda Mary Mastern

The Hayloft

We had a barn with a hayloft
Where we used to play.
It was such a perfect place
When it was filled with hay.

From the tips of the rafters
We could swiftly slide,
Or we would tunnel deep inside
And from the others hide.

The fragrance of the sun-dried hay
Filled the big old barn
Where we loved to sit around
And spin a scary yarn.

On rainy days, we loved best
To slip to the hayloft to play.
Sunshine seemed to fill the barn
As we romped in the golden hay.

Many years have long gone by
Since we played in the hay.
But I remember the old barn loft
Where we would play all day.

Sharon Rose Davison

Tom Sawyer

Saturday morning was come, and all the summer world was bright and fresh and brimming with life.

Tom appeared on the sidewalk with a bucket of whitewash and a long-handled brush. He surveyed the fence. All gladness left him and a deep melancholy settled down upon his spirit. Thirty yards of board fence nine feet high! Life to him seemed hollow, and existence but a burden. Sighing, he dipped his brush and passed along the topmost plank. He repeated the operation; did it again; compared the insignificant whitewashed streak with the far-reaching continent of unwhitewashed fence, and sat down on a tree-box discouraged.

Tom began to think of the fun he had planned for this day, and his sorrows mul-tiplied. Soon the free boys would come tripping along on all sorts of delicious expeditions, and they would make fun of him for having to work. The very thought of it burnt him like fire. He got out his worldly wealth and examined it—bits of toys, marbles, and trash; enough to buy an exchange of *work*, maybe, but not half enough to buy so much as half an hour of pure freedom. So he returned his

meager means to his pocket, and gave up the idea of trying to buy the boys.

At this dark and hopeless moment an inspiration burst upon him! It was nothing less than a great, magnificent inspiration. Tom took up his brush and went tranquilly to work.

Ben Rogers hove in sight presently—the very boy, of all boys, whose ridicule he had been dreading. Ben was eating an apple, and giving a long, melodious whoop, at intervals, followed by a deep-toned ding-dong-dong, ding-dong-dong, for he was personating a steamboat. As Ben drew near, he slackened speed.

Tom went on whitewashing and paid no attention to the steamboat.

Ben stared a moment and then said, *"Hi-yi! You're a stump, ain't you!"*

No answer. Tom surveyed his last touch with the eye of an artist; then he gave his brush another gentle sweep and surveyed the result, as before.

Ben ranged up alongside of him.

Tom's mouth watered for the apple, but he stuck to his work.

Ben said, "Hello, old chap, you got to work, hey?"

Tom wheeled suddenly and said, "Why, it's you, Ben! I warn't noticing."

"Say—*I'm* going in a-swimming, I am. Don't you wish you could? But of course you'd druther *work*—wouldn't you? Course you would!"

Tom contemplated the boy a bit, and said, "What do you call work?"

"Why, ain't *that* work?"

Tom resumed his whitewashing, and answered carelessly, " Well, maybe it is, and maybe it ain't. All I know is, it suits Tom Sawyer. Does a boy get a chance to white-wash a fence every day?"

That put the thing in a new light. Ben stopped nibbling his apple.

Tom swept his brush daintily back and forth—stepped back to note the effect—added a touch here and there—criticized the effect again.

Ben was watching every move and getting more and more interested, more and more absorbed. Presently he said, "Say, Tom, let *me* whitewash a little."

Tom considered, was about to consent; but he changed his mind. "Ben, I'd like to, honest injun. Jim wanted to do it, too, but Aunt Polly wouldn't let him. "You see, Aunt Polly's awful particular about this fence—right here on the street, you know. If it was the back fence I wouldn't mind and *she* wouldn't. Yes, she's awful particular about this fence. It's got to be done very careful. I reckon there ain't one boy in a thousand, maybe two thousand, that can do it the way it's got to be done."

"No—is that so? Oh come, now—lemme just try. Only just a little—I'd let *you*, if you was me, Tom."

"Now don't you see how I'm fixed? If you was to tackle this fence and anything was to happen to it—"

"Oh shucks, I'll be just as careful. Now lemme try. Say—I'll give you the core of my apple."

"Well, here. No, Ben, now don't. I'm afraid—"

"I'll give you *all* of it!"

Tom gave up the brush with reluctance in his face but eagerness in his heart. And while Ben worked and sweated in the sun, the artist sat on a barrel in the shade close by, dangled his legs, munched his apple, and planned the slaughter of more innocents.

There was no lack of material; and when the middle of the afternoon came, from being a poor, poverty-stricken boy in the morning, Tom was literally rolling in wealth. He had twelve marbles, a jew's-harp, a piece of blue bottle glass to look through, a spool cannon, a key that wouldn't unlock anything, a fragment of chalk, a glass stopper of a decanter, a tin soldier, a couple of tadpoles, six firecrackers, a kitten with only one eye, a brass doorknob, a dog collar—but no dog—the handle of a knife, four pieces of orange-peel, and a dilapidated old window-sash.

He had a nice, good, idle time all the while—plenty of company—and the fence had three coats of whitewash on it! If he hadn't run out of whitewash, he would have bankrupted every boy in the village.

Tom said to himself that it was not such a hollow world after all. He had discovered a great law of human action without knowing it—namely, that in order to make a man or boy covet a thing, it is necessary to make the thing difficult to attain. If he had been a great and wise philosopher, like the writer of this story, he would now have comprehended that work consists of whatever a body is *obliged* to do, and that play consists of whatever a body is not obliged to do.

Mark Twain

From *Tom Sawyer* by Mark Twain, illustrated by Toby Bluth, copyright© 1985 by Toby Bluth. Published by Ideals Publishing, Nashville, Tennessee.

A Doll of Yesterday

Delicate porcelain features
Hand-painted hair and eyes;
She cannot say "mama,"
Nor can she laugh or cry.

Her lips are like a rosebud.
Her cloth body so soft to hold.
She has no batteries to make her walk.
She was not cast from a plastic mold.

Her gown is hand-stitched,
Trimmed with the finest lace.
Her bonnet adds a special touch
To the already perfect face.

She cannot do the modern things
That dolls can do today.
But with a little more pretending
She is just as fun in every way.

Patra Giroux

Old Dolls

Old dolls are links in history
To styles of the past,
To memories of years gone by
That manage still to last.

There were china dolls and peddler dolls
And dolls of hand-carved wood,
Dolls of bisque and dolls of straw
So dear to our childhood.

I like the way old dolls are dressed;
I like their shape and size,
But I like most the expressions
That I find within their eyes.

The eyes just seem to speak to me,
Undimmed by passing years;
They've traversed generations with
Expressions bright and clear.

Craig Sathoff

Folk Songs

I love old songs with simple tunes,
    And words that common people know,
That have been handed down the years,
    And have a rhythm and a flow,
The sound of joyful dancing feet
    The rise and fall of a drummer's beat.

Songs of the people gay and strong,
    Of lover's meetings, sad farewells,
Feast days and days of special grace,
    The sound of holy Christmas bells,
Sounding across the fields of white,
    Like angels' voices in the night.

I love the songs of harvest time,
    That hold within each glad refrain
The lilt of wind across the hills,
    The sound of reapers in the grain,
Stout wagon wheels that lurch along,
    The magic of the shepherds' song.

A roundelay, a choir's chant,
    Band music floating overhead;
A small girl singing to her doll,
    A mother putting a child to bed.
Songs of comfort and of cheer,
    That common people love to hear.

Old songs that have a tale to tell,
Of love and joy, peace and farewell.

Edna Jaques

Photo Opposite
MUSIC OF HOME
Mack and Betty Kelley

Country Chronicle

A ninety-year-old neighbor continues a custom that was once commonplace in rural America. She wears a sunbonnet, chin ribbon and all, when she is out in the sun. Many memories are rekindled when we see her out in the yard.

We know her as Annie, a pert and prim lady who lives across the road from where she started housekeeping nearly seventy years ago. She has always called the country her paradise in the universe. Her home is her haven of content. She wouldn't trade her solacing sanctuary of bird songs and blooms, of fresh air, sunshine and rain, or of moonlight and stars, for any mansion in the finest city in the world.

Annie doesn't go to the gardens anymore to pick sweet corn and tomatoes, peas and green beans, or berries in season. Instead,

she makes sure she will have the beauty and
fragrance of blossoms near her doorstep
from the first tender flowers of spring well
into autumn when frost stings the blooms.

We stop to chat with Annie every week.
Her bonnet is a standard trademark, sym-
bolic of a long life, and of earlier years when
most farm housewives wore their bonnets
when working in the gardens of summer. (I
am reminded of my own mother who took
me along as a child to pick wild strawberries
in the thinning meadows of June.)

Annie is familiar with every acre of the
countryside about her. She knows it at
sunrise and at sunset. Although she is in the
sunset of her own life, her bright outlook
and her cheerful optimism are as inspiring as
the splendor of the rising sun over the
eastern hills.

Lansing Christman

Jack-of-All-Trades

Oh, how we need a man like this
Within our town today,
The friendly, able fix-it man
We knew those yesterdays.

He'd mend our screens and trim our shrubs
Or help with gardening.
He'd build, repair, or scrub, or paint.
He'd do most anything.

He loved to help his fellow man.
His joy was in his work.
No task would seem too much for him,
And never would he shirk.

He had a way of bettering
Most anything he'd touch.
Oh, how I'd like to call him now.
I miss him very much.

Craig E. Sathoff

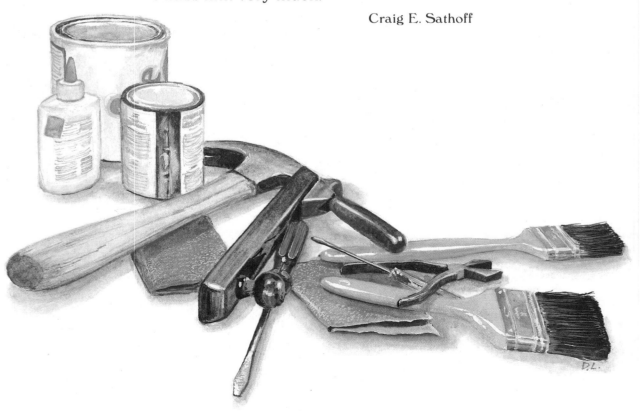

Photo Opposite
THE BROOM MAKER
Arnold J. Kaplan
Berg and Associates

Ship
of Dreams

Long before I grew so tall,
In times when I had no cares at all,
Adventure came in a flannel cap
With a dusty sweater and a welcome lap.

Upon my Grandpa's knee I'd climb
To take a trip to the shelf of time.
He'd clear his throat, then, by the by,
He'd start his tales with a twinkling eye.
And off to magic lands we'd soar
Through fabled days past history's door.

Or future lore he'd often borrow,
A thrilling yarn from some tomorrow.
Up, up we'd go, then quickly down,
On a roller coaster through the town,
Yet never to the same place twice...
We'd sail, I'd drift, my dreams so nice!

I cried that day I climbed the knee
To find that lap too small for me—
To know that ship might sail no more,
And strand me here on native shore...

But Grandpa's kept things well in hand,
Still travels to his far off land—
With a new generation on that lap
Near the dusty sweater and the flannel cap...

And me, I'm now a stowaway
As the vessel thrills its crew each day—
My children love those flowing sails
Of Grandpa's ship...
And his wondrous tales...

C.L. Serra

Country Auction

The old familiar auction sale
Is such a heap of fun.
Come, Maude, we are already late,
The auction has begun.

There stands the clever auctioneer,
A witty soul is he;
He knows that when the people laugh
They buy more readily!

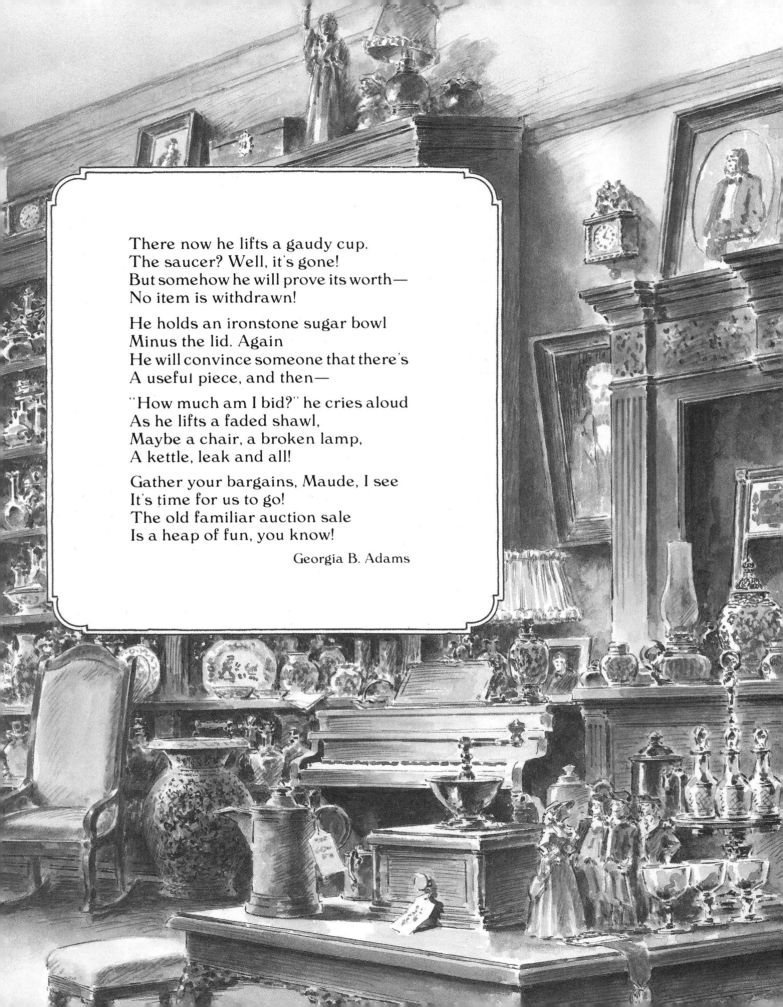

There now he lifts a gaudy cup.
The saucer? Well, it's gone!
But somehow he will prove its worth—
No item is withdrawn!

He holds an ironstone sugar bowl
Minus the lid. Again
He will convince someone that there's
A useful piece, and then—

"How much am I bid?" he cries aloud
As he lifts a faded shawl,
Maybe a chair, a broken lamp,
A kettle, leak and all!

Gather your bargains, Maude, I see
It's time for us to go!
The old familiar auction sale
Is a heap of fun, you know!

Georgia B. Adams

Cabin in the Mountains

There's a cabin in the mountains
'Neath a sheltering rocky peak,
And its brown thatched roof is hidden
As the pines take on retreat.

Just below this point of vantage,
There's a trout stream floating by,
And its echo in the woodland
Meets "Big Sandy" beneath the sky.

There the trout come out to mingle
With the pike out in the pond
As we don our boots and tackle
And go out to look around.

To this cabin in the mountains
We go back from year to year,
And carry home the memories
That we cherish and hold dear.

Edith M. Helstern

Bright Weather

I love bright weather when the fields are green,
When every garden tries to steal the scene,
Flaunting its loveliness with tender pride,
And Earth takes on the raiment of a bride.

I love bright weather with a touch of rain
To gladden up the fields and wash the grain
'Till every leaf shines like a warrior's blade,
And fields are like a carpet richly laid.

I love bright weather when the skies bend down
To touch the little houses of the town;
When red-cheeked apples and sweet Bartlett pears
Send out their messages like signal flares;

When wheat has taken on its golden coat,
And there is rapture in the robin's note;
When purple haze hangs like a temple veil
Along the upper reaches of the trail.

I love bright weather . . . sown with stars and song.
And shadows on the stubble blue and long
Like ladders stretching out along the ground,
Showing the world where peace might still be found.

Edna Jaques

A Summer Day

This day is made for dreaming
And gazing on a view
Of magic white cloud-ships
Sailing skies of summer blue.

A day to seek a hill of green
Bathed in golden sun,
And rest awhile beneath a tree
Till stars peek one by one.

A day to hear the songs of birds
Winging gaily by,
And look up at the treetops
So stately and so high.

A day to see the fragrant flowers
Nod proudly on their stems.
Fresh and sweet the breeze and earth
Are priceless, precious gems.

You'll find your cares will disappear
Because the sky and sod
Hold many wonders for your heart
For they are gifts from God.

LaVerne P. Larson

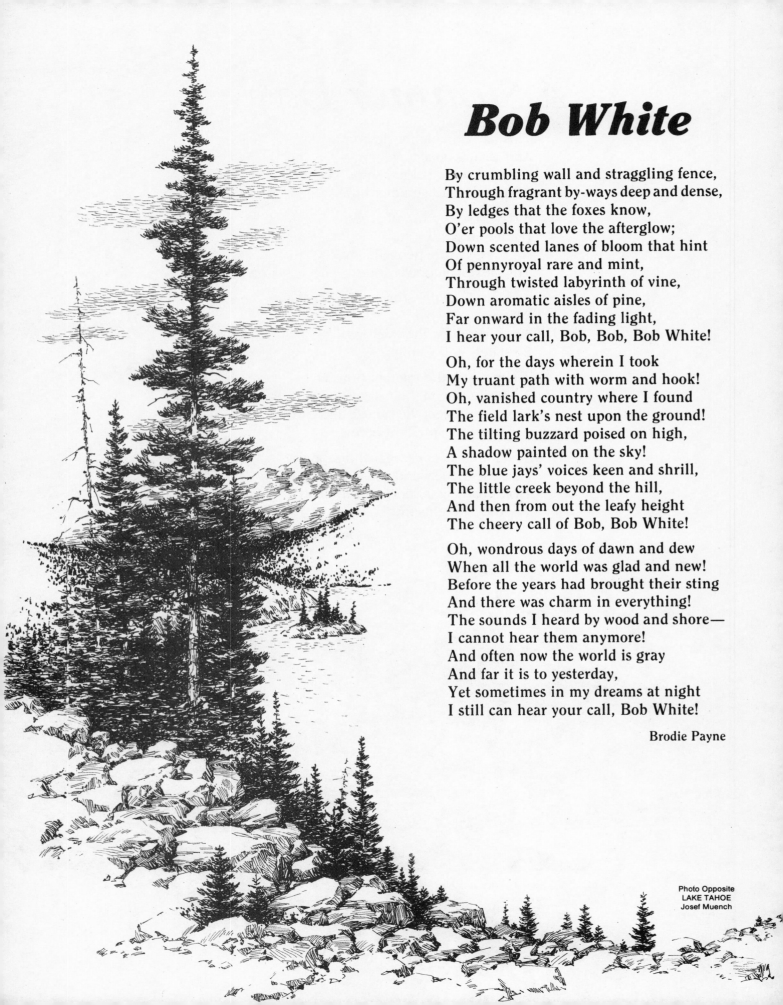

Bob White

By crumbling wall and straggling fence,
Through fragrant by-ways deep and dense,
By ledges that the foxes know,
O'er pools that love the afterglow;
Down scented lanes of bloom that hint
Of pennyroyal rare and mint,
Through twisted labyrinth of vine,
Down aromatic aisles of pine,
Far onward in the fading light,
I hear your call, Bob, Bob, Bob White!

Oh, for the days wherein I took
My truant path with worm and hook!
Oh, vanished country where I found
The field lark's nest upon the ground!
The tilting buzzard poised on high,
A shadow painted on the sky!
The blue jays' voices keen and shrill,
The little creek beyond the hill,
And then from out the leafy height
The cheery call of Bob, Bob White!

Oh, wondrous days of dawn and dew
When all the world was glad and new!
Before the years had brought their sting
And there was charm in everything!
The sounds I heard by wood and shore—
I cannot hear them anymore!
And often now the world is gray
And far it is to yesterday,
Yet sometimes in my dreams at night
I still can hear your call, Bob White!

Brodie Payne

Photo Opposite
LAKE TAHOE
Josef Muench

Katherine Edelman

Katherine Edelman was seventeen when she left Ireland to make her home in the United States. Her writing career began when the first poem she submitted was published by the *Kansas City Star*. Mrs. Edelman's poems have a very special lilt. This lyrical ability made the writing of verse and lighter forms of poetry a pleasure to her, and she always found ready markets for her work. She was widely published in leading periodicals in the United States and abroad, and her work has been included in many collections and anthologies. Many of her poems have been used on greeting cards, and several have been successfully put to music. "The Lane to Ballybree," which was set to music by Oley Speaks, is from her book *Shamrock and Prairie Grass*. The book's title reflected her affection for Ireland and the United States, the land of her birth and her adopted homeland. The book is filled with the gentleness and understanding for which Katherine Edelman was known.

Books

My shelf of books! I love them so!
They take me where I want to go.

Adventure, deeds of every age
Lie captured on the printed page;
Through them I hear the swish of seas,
The wind in lofty mountain trees.
Their magic brings before my gaze
Heroes of stirring, ancient days.
Here in my chair, through day or night,
They lend me wings for daring flight.

I love my shelf of books, they are
Pathways to sun...and moon...and star!

Pumpkin Yellow

See that yellow pumpkin
Ripening in the sun?
Let's take it over in the shade,
And have a lot of fun!

Let's open it with special care,
Then with a heavy spoon
Scoop out its tasty, juicy heart,
That's yellow like the moon.

And then while Mother makes the pies
Of crusty, golden brown,
We'll carve it till its hollow shell
Looks like a funny clown.

Careful Builders

Outside my window
Birds debate
About the building
Of a nest

Through the morning hours.
Forgetting song,
They study what
Is wisest, best.

Then, with decision,
Widely roam
To gather makings
For their home.

At Easter

The promise of eternal spring
Is with us strong today.
We see it in the budding tree,
In every walk and way.
The earth is blossoming again
With newborn beauty bright,
And winter's gloom has vanished
In sunlight warm and bright.

The trees that stood so stark and bare
With bursting buds are filled.
The little brook is singing now
The song that long was stilled.
New verdure springs in every field.
The violets shyly peep
And all the earth in joy awakes
From its long winter sleep.

How meet it is that Eastertime
Should greet us with the spring,
When newborn hope and life and breath
Is filling everything;
When all the earth and sky proclaim
The truth He gave to men,
That after death's encircling sleep
They, too, would rise again.

Firelight and Friendship

With firelight glowing on the hearth,
Shades drawn against dull weather,
Few things are more delightful
Than breaking bread together.
Where easy, happy comradeship
With food and firelight blend,
The hour holds special gladness
When shared by friend and friend.

Country Stream

This lovely stream
So country-free
Now skirts a hill,
Now skips a tree.
Then, leaving shade
Where willows toss
Their gray-green leaves,
It runs across

A slanting meadow
Daisy-starred,
Then lingers by
A near farmyard
Where, after seeming
Rest, once more
It turns and twists on
As before.

Motherhood

Tonight dreams reach so wide, so high,
They touch the moon, the stars, the sky;
Incoming tides with richest store
Are mine—I own the world, and more—
Tonight within my arms, close pressed,
Our little son lies on my breast.

Summer

Summer is a little boy
With sunny hair of gold,
So carefree and so wonderful
With magic to unfold.

All the world is brighter
And happier it seems,
And there is time for fun,
Laughter and new dreams.

Dusty, winding country roads
Lined with wild flowers,
Swimming, boating, picnics
To wile away the hours.

White clouds like ships a-sail
In a sky of deepest blue,
Sunsets tinged in rose and gold
And dawns of pinkest hue.

Nights of starlit beauty
That wear a silver crown,
And you know that God is watching
Over every sleeping town.

Summer is a little boy
With a twinkle in his eye,
And a merry smile on his lips
As each lovely day draws nigh.

LaVerne P. Larson

June Wonders

How lovely are the bright June days
With meadowlands so green,
With golden sun and bright blue sky,
And the countryside serene.

Wild flowers bloom beside the lane,
And willows shade the creek
Where wild ferns grow in shadowed glade,
And the water is cool and deep.

The days of June are rare indeed,
For balmy breezes blow
And gently rock the leafy boughs
Where birdlings nest and grow.

Come out amid the bright green world
With all the earth in tune,
Enjoy the magic wonder of
The lovely month of June.

Mildred L. Jarrell

Photo Opposite
SPRING BANQUET
Nancy Anne Dawe

Wild
Berries

Wild berries are beyond a doubt
My favorite fruits of all,
So every June I start the search
That lasts till nearly fall.

Wild strawberries may not be as plump
As the commercial kind,
But a sweeter and more luscious taste
Is rather hard to find.

And, oh, what joy in hunting them
Through fields of ripening grain,
Beside the creek, 'long fence-row paths,
And in the meadow's shade.

Wild raspberries grow along the fence
In one of Grandpa's fields,
And every summer I await
The ripening of their yield.

What follows then is true delight
With homemade jam and pie,
And ice cream sundaes cool and sweet
With berries piled up high.

For years I've gone a-berrying;
For years I've found my fill
Of luscious berries, homemade treats,
And hikes through wooded hills.

Craig Sathoff

Sing a Song of Summer

Sing a song of summer. . .
Of blue sky overhead,
Of emerald carpet on the lawn,
Of berries ripe and red.

Sing a song of summer. . .
Of cornstalks stretching up,
Of fence rows lined with wild rose,
Of bee and buttercup.

Sing a song of summer. . .
Of thumb-sized crimson beet,
Of fresh-pulled crispy radishes,
Of new peas, sugar sweet.

Sing a song of summer. . .
A thankful melody
For all the gifts a summer day
Bestows on you and me.

Virginia Blanck Moore

Sounds of Summer

How delightful is the music
Of lovely summer days,
When flute-like notes of trilling birds
Greet the sun's first golden rays.

A flying chorus of golden bees
Hum a buzzing roundelay,
And green leaves dance so lightly
In a summertime ballet.

The winds that sing in the treetops,
Like obligato from on high,
Blend their voices with the crickets
In a twilight lullaby.

How full of peace this world could be
If it would sing in tune
With all the sweet and peaceful sounds
Of a summer afternoon.

Dorothy F. Fischler

We Want Your Friendship

Do you remember the saying, "Make new friends, but keep the old—one is silver, the other gold"? We do, and in our next issue, Friendship Ideals, we celebrate the joys which friendship brings to all of us. As a preview, we would like to share the way one of our friends, Mrs. Nellie Beel, of St. Louis, Missouri, feels about Ideals.

> If you've had a busy, heavy day,
> And it has been quite taxing,
> Pick up an ideals® magazine.
> You'll find it so relaxing.
>
> Its beauty will invade your soul
> And cares will fall away.
> It's like a breath of fresh, clean air
> At the end of a weary day.
>
> Your heart will fill with gratitude
> As you see lovely things
> Our God has created,
> Of which all nature sings.
>
> So give yourself an ideals® treat
> Before you're lying down to sleep.
> Your soul will feel so calm and sweet,
> And there will come such rest and peace.

Thank you, Mrs. Beel! Everyone can enjoy such a relaxing treat or share one with a friend by starting a gift subscription with Friendship Ideals.

ACKNOWLEDGEMENTS

Our sincere thanks to the following people whose addresses we were unable to locate: Ruby Pearl Coffman for COUNTRY VILLAGE; Sharon Rose Davison for THE HAYLOFT; Brodie Payne for BOB WHITE from his book YOUR FOLKS AND MINE, copyright 1926; and William Arnette Wofford for WOOD THRUSH from his book A QUIET ROAD, Harbinger House, copyright 1943.